ANXIETY MAKES ME ANXIOUS

Written by: Shayna Brazier
Illustrated by: Jake Bush

For permission requests please contact: Shayna Brazier at:
AnxietyMakesMeAnxious@gmail.com

Printed in the United States of America

First Printing, 2017

Library of Congress Control Number: 2017902279
ISBN 978-0-9987247-0-6

The Happiness Center
1106 E. Rogen Way
Superior, CO 80027

www.thehappinesscenter.com

DEDICATION

I dedicate this book to myself for going through all that pain and anxiety that inspired such a masterpiece.

Just kidding, I dedicate it to everyone who has helped me live a full and happy and anxious life including: my husband and kids, my family, my friends, nurses and doctors, flight attendants, forest rangers, grocery clerks, inventor of Xanax, meteorologists, engineers and therapists

TABLE OF CONTENTS

INTRODUCTION

Anxiety is like gas. All of us have a little of it and some of us have a lot of it. It can make going to social events a little harder but when the dust settles and the moments pass, we can look back on them and realize that they are so, so funny. If you are reading this then you probably have anxiety, know someone who struggles with anxiety, help someone who lives with anxiety, or you live in a cave on another planet. There is a plethora of serious books about anxiety and the different things you can do to ease this disorder. They tell you that there is hope, and that with the help of the author (who is also a doctor) you will overcome this horrible plight and come out a survivor. This is NOT one of those books, although I have read and loved many of those. If you expect this book to give you therapeutic advice on how to cure your anxiety in 50 simple steps, then you are going to be disappointed. On the other hand, if you want to have a good laugh to spite your worries and feel a little more normal and slightly less psycho about your anxiety then read on! Also if you don't worry very much, or worry just a little and need ideas about what new things to worry about, then be relieved that your investment of $35 at Barnes and Nobles, or heaven forbid 25 cents at the nearest garage sale, was well worth it.

Anxiety can be crippling. It can make you want to give up on all the things that you love. It can make you want to cut yourself off from loved ones, acquaintances, and total strangers. It can literally make you—literally, not figuratively, literally— depressed and tired. *Man this book is making me depressed.* Is there any hope at all? If not, that would be a short book, and a long lawsuit. The answer is yes! There is hope! You can have your anxiety and eat it too—I mean live life too. Is this easier said than done? Of course it is! Everything that is worth it is easier said than done. The thing that I hate the most about anxiety is that it has somehow become this very sad and sheltered disorder... which it is, but that doesn't mean that it is not also incredibly funny. I think that anxiety makes for the best stories! Going on a trip to let's say a haunted forest with "normal" people—normal. Going to this forest with someone who has anxiety—hilarious. How do I know this? I have anxiety. I go on trips. This makes me an expert on the matter.

A hero of mine, Marjorie Hinckley, once said, "The only way to get through life is to laugh your way through it. You either have to laugh or cry. I prefer to laugh. Crying gives me a headache."On that note, here is a little glimpse into my life with anxiety. There is no one better than myself to share this story since I have been with myself with anxiety my whole life.

Whoever said that there is 'nothing to fear but fear itself' was not very creative. Off the top of my head, without even blinking, I can think of 10 really good things to fear and about 25 more mediocre ones. You see, I was born a worrier. Have you ever noticed how worrier and warrior are so close? I'm pretty sure I was meant to be a warrior, but somewhere in my DNA I was supposed to have two red segments and a blue, and I ended up with two blues and a red or something crazy like that. Either way, while most babies were enjoying the lullabies of soothing amniotic fluid, I'm pretty sure I was worrying about the chord cutting off my air supply or my feet coming out first. Yes, I was a very intelligent fetus.

My parents told me that one of the funniest things was sitting me up next to a tissue when I was a baby. They would blow on it causing it to move and I would freak out (this was obviously before parents got overly scrutinized for every 'character building' prank). I grew up in a "normal" family in a "normal" town. I have two brothers and one sister, some of whom have anxiety as well. I don't remember feeling "different" as a kid because, like I said, anxiety has ALWAYS been a part of my life.

I have a vivid memory of getting a sled for Christmas one year, and my sister and I went to sit on it in the living room. For the purpose of slowing down, there was a foot lever on the sled made of plastic. My sister went to step on it and I lunged at her. I was convinced that she would start that sled and we would fly right through the wall into the kitchen. Pretty much any time we would do something fun, I would worry about a tragic outcome... but I would still do it, mostly because my mom and dad made me and partially because my need to love life was heavy enough to tip the scales in favor of fun. If we were going skiing, the chair lift cable could snap and we could plummet to the ground. At the water parks, I would be on the lookout for people drowning at the bottom of the wave pools. When we went on road trips, I would stare out the front window, partially so I wouldn't get car sick and partially to pay attention to the traffic in case I needed to alert my dad to something out of the ordinary. I had anxiety way before I knew what anxiety was, and way way before it was so widely talked about.

Somewhere along the line, I earned the title of "worry wart." I tried to change that to "concerned crusader" or "vigilant viking," but worry wart is what stuck, and I've proudly carried that label ever since. You see, in my mind worriers aren't freaks, people with no fears are freaks! How can you be afraid of nothing?

MY FIRST PANIC ATTACK

Much like a first kiss or a first car, I have a place in my heart for my first true panic attack (right

next to first broken bone and first public vomiting).
I was in my early twenties and had just moved to
Denver with my husband Drew and our 5-month
old daughter. Ironically, Drew was going to grad
school for a doctorate in Clinical Psychology. I told
Drew that because he wasn't crazy enough to be
a shrink (come on, we ALL know that shrinks are
cray cray), he needed to marry me to be able to
have personal experience with the psycho things
he was about to learn. Anyways, that summer
was particularly challenging because we moved
to Denver a semester early for a summer job that
Drew had lined up.

When we arrived with our yearlong lease signed
and our 8x6 Uhaul in tow, we discovered that
the summer job fell through. This was right after
undergrad so our savings were equivalent to a
week's worth of food—and I'm talking like Ramen
for dinner kind of food. Naturally we took the first
gig we could find and quickly found ourselves
putting DirectTV flyers on door handles for 8 cents
a flyer. I know what you're thinking: this must have
been in the 1970s. Nope, this was 2008. I would
push our baby in the stroller up one side of the
street while Drew rollerbladed—once again 2008,
not the 90s—down the other side and up to meet
me. Our first 4 hour day (we were limited on what

neighborhoods we could do every day) yielded a whopping $40. *Why is she telling us this story? This has nothing to do with panic attacks.*

Needless to say, we were tired and a little stressed financially. Our beautiful baby girl was such a joy.... . and so much work that when I also found out we were expecting a second child so soon, despite the birth control, I may not have been beaming with excitement. I discovered that being totally overwhelmed gives the illusion of beaming/glowing as well. So here we were: young, broke, expecting a surprise baby, and about to start grad school. I was at my limit when a member of our clergy called and wanted to talk. Hooray! My prayers had been answered! I just knew that we were going to get offered a million dollars and a live-in nanny, since that's exactly what I needed and therefore exactly what I had been praying for. We stepped into the meeting and the clergyman said, "The Lord would like to bless you..." *Here it comes... come on nanny!* "He would like you to serve this congregation by allowing Drew to help direct the flock... for free... while you, Shayna, support and sustain him by being alone most of Sunday and tackling 2 children—scratch that, 2 babies in a pew on your own." At least that's what I heard him say. What? I didn't pray for

ANXIETY MAKES ME ANXIOUS

'mo' problems. I prayed for money... and a nanny! I would have even taken a manny, as long as he wasn't too good looking. But there it was: the offer to become better people. And since we've already established that I am quite insane, we did the only natural thing and accepted the offer.

The next day at Sunday services as they announced this change to the congregation and asked everyone to raise their hand in support of this change, I had my first, real, true panic attack. Spinning head, sweaty palms, rapid heart rate, shallow breaths, and all the works! I literally stood up and walked out of the room while the announcement was being made because I wanted to pass out in the hallway instead of the chapel. To this day I think I am the only person who didn't raise my hand in agreement of the change. That day, panic attacks became the thorned edges on my brillo blanket of anxiety. It was like I had figured out a way to bottle up enough anxiety so that if I was shaken just right, I would explode with reactions. In the world of soda pop and antacids this is very fun. In the world of anxiety and panic, not so much.

Many people who have anxiety also develop depression. I see how this can happen: If anxiety takes over and starts calling the shots in your life, then a lot of the fun things stop happening. Fortunately (and knock on wood), my anxiety has not yielded that result. In psychoanalyzing myself, I'm pretty sure I have a deep rooted Freudian rebellious side. That, or I got some serious second year syndrome by editing all of Drew's Psychology papers in grad school, because I have diagnosed myself with a very mild case of Oppositional Defiant Disorder, but instead of my hatred of authority being directed at my parents, the government, and police, it has all been directed at my anxiety. I would just call it Anxiety Defiant Disorder, but ADD has already been taken and is quite popular. How do I think this ODD of anxiety affects my life? For example, if I had been alive for the American Revolution, I would have been a Minute (wo)Man—a frightened ineffective one, but I would have signed up nonetheless. In the French Revolution I would have marched on Versailles—ok maybe I would have cheered on the marchers while I volunteered to stay back and watch the kids. In WWII, I would have been hiding Anne Franke's cousins—or at least baking bread for my neighbors who were helping her. And I would have gladly participated in the underground railroad—and by participated I mean lie about its existence by claiming that I'm always sweaty and guilty-looking, and frankly the townspeople would've believed it.

So maybe I'm not hard core rebellious but I do like to "live and let live," including letting myself live, which is why I've fought tooth and nail against my anxiety. I can literally see all of you therapists reading this cringing, since I am well aware that we are supposed to "let the anxiety be, don't fight it, don't give it energy or power." As an expert on anxiety and a life devoted to being a case study for it, I respectfully disagree. I just don't think that having a campfire relationship with my anxiety is the goal. *Kumbaya anxiety, Kumbaya.* I would much rather be on Holiday, Billie Holiday that is, about it: *The way I wear my hat, the way I sip my tea... no anxiety can't take that away from me.* So I look my anxiety in the face and I get angry and then I laugh. Ok, sometimes I cry. Ok, many times I cry, but sometimes that crying turns into laughter, a crying laughing mix, including blotchy red cheeks and all, of outward expression which is as close to curing my anxiety as I'm probably gonna get. And I'm ok with that. While I am not narcissistic enough to pretend that my solution will work for everyone, I hope that it helps someone. Even anxiety can become a strength. *"Use the force Luke."* You can recognize the fear, push it, and still live the life you want, or the life you want to want. While the idea of not worrying and just being happy makes for a catchy tune, it's rubbish. You don't have to eliminate worry to be happy. They can coexist, mostly peacefully (like Canada and USA peacefully: snarky bantering, but peaceful coexistence). I'm going to go ahead and get off my soap box now and get to the meat of this non-therapeutic yet highly entertaining book.

CHAPTER 1: FLYING

"The bulk of mankind is as well equipped for flying as thinking."
-Jonathon Swift

If I had to pick my biggest fear, also called an anxiety trigger—see I did learn something proofing all those papers—it would be flying. But in all honesty, picking my biggest fear is like choosing my favorite child: virtually impossible. This is a conundrum for me because I love to travel. Scratch that, I love to be somewhere new; the traveling part I could live without. Living away from family gave me plenty of opportunities to become well acquainted with my fear of flying. This fear has evolved into a fear of being in the airport for a flight, fear of driving to the airport to fly, fear of packing for the purpose of going to the airport

to fly, and fear of thinking about the flight or any possible future flight. While I have never been on a pleasant flight, I will share just one experience.

One Christmas my glorious parents announced that they were gifting us all (kids, spouses, and grandkids) with an all-expenses paid, week-long trip to Hawaii. While everyone cheered and shouted hooray, I immediately thought:

Hawaii=flight
Flight= flying over water
Flying over water=point of no return
Point of no return=certain death

The second announcement was that we had 9 months to prepare for it: aka, 9 months to worry about it. This is time for approximately 5,000 conversations with myself that go:

> **Me:** *You're a worrier!*

> **Me:** *No, I'm a warrior this will be fun.*

> **Me:** *No, you're a worrier.*

> **Me:** *No, I'm a warrior I love Hawaii.*

> **Me:** *No, you're a worrier.*

> **Me:** *NO, I'M A WARRIOR and I'm gonna prove it to you!! (rebellious side coming through)*

So I had 9 months to figure out how to survive a 6 hour flight to Hawaii. For the first time, I thought that maybe I should seek professional help. Technically living with Drew is professional help, but he was a 2nd year grad student at the time, and I thought this flight required the help of a 4th year student—and yes I, too, think it's absurd that this was the first time I sought professional help. So naturally being a poor student wife, I called the free school clinic to be the guinea pig for a budding therapist before they go into the real world and can potentially screw up real people paying with real money. I had the sweetest student who we will call Edyta, because that's her name and I'm pretty sure she'll never read this because this is not a real therapy book and has little to no therapeutic value (but just in case, hey Edyta, what's up girl!).

I went in to get help with my fear of flying and ended up talking about my anxiety in general. She went through the typical deep breathing techniques, as well as the "watch your thoughts float down the river to put you in the here and now versus the future" techniques, both of which honestly I still use today, more for the "my kid just spilled his milk all over my bedspread that I just washed and I need to calm down" moments than the sheer panic moments. On that tangent, why aren't they teaching you "How To Deal With Stress 101" in conjunction with the "How To File Your Taxes and Other Useful Things You Actually Need To Know"in High School? Heaven knows our teachers are experts on both since we don't pay them enough to afford weekly massages and a CPA.

Where was I? Apparently I also have ADD, or ADHD and yes, I know there is a difference but to the masses of us they are basically the same. Anyway, Edyta: she really was so sweet. As I got closer and closer to the flight, my fears and anxiety got deeper and more aggressive. At one point, Edyta asked me what the very worst thing that could happen was. I think she was expecting me to say "death," because I am not an amateur worrier; death is definitely not the worst thing that could happen. This is why when people say, "you know your chances of dying in a car crash on the way to the airport are exponentially higher than dying in a plane crash," the point is moot—which as a side note, why would you tell someone who worries as a living that there are things to worry about that they hadn't considered? That's like going up to the homeless guy and saying 'you know your life is pretty sad, but it would be sadder if you went ahead and did drugs and sold your body for money while you're at it'. Anxiety is not a forest fire, you don't fight fear with fear...you fight it with anger and ugly crying laughter.

Where was I? Oh yes, 'what is the worst thing that could happen?' So I proceeded to tell her."The worst thing that could happen is that we are flying over the ocean and the plane starts to go down. Because, for some unknown reason we are way way *way* up in the sky, this means we have a full 60 seconds—ok 45 seconds minimum to plummet towards the earth. While plummeting, the centrifugal force rips my lap child off my lap and smashes his head into the overhead bin. Because someone is likely out of their seat, they come crashing into my son and force him to fly to the back of the plane bruised and bloody as I try to reach for him unsuccessfully. As I am doing so, a piece of debris rips off my arms and I don't have time to bleed to death so I use the last 30 seconds of my life being horrified beyond repair that I can't get to my son with blood oozing out of my chopped off limbs and then we crash and die and no one ever finds our remains because the impact annihilated them." Then I looked up. Edyta's eyes were so wide, and slightly terrified. I cannot believe that I actually told her my real worst case scenario. I should have gone with death.

What was I thinking? *Death is good. Death is easy.* I should have said death. *Crap. Isn't she a mandatory reporter? She probably thinks I'm a psychopath. What if she reports me and they take away my children? What if she tells Drew and he doesn't let me be alone with the children anymore? What if she, what if, what if, what if?* Things were getting out of control. I did the only thing that I could think of. I blurted out "I AM NOT A PSYCHOPATH!" Oh ya Shayna, that's how you convince her. I continued, "just in case you thought I was, I'm not." I'm pretty sure I made Edyta rethink her career path that day, or at least her decision to ever ask anyone what the worst case scenario could be. While therapy was helping me label and organize my disorders, the fear of the impending flight did not go away.

Alas, the week of the flight of doom and despair—I mean trip had come. I usually don't medicate myself for everyday anxiety (I am just so fun to be around I would hate for the people around me to miss out on that) but I do take an exception for flying. As I was packing, I dug into the back of the medicine cabinet looking for my little blue pills of relief. Just as I reached the bottle, I knew something was wrong. This feels way too light. I don't hear the jiggle jiggle of pills bumping into each other and as I hastily opened the bottle my suspicions were confirmed. I. Was. Out. How was I out?? True I only use them when I fly. True I only fly once a year or so. But still, how was I out? I quickly called the BOX. What is the BOX you ask? Think of a huge insurance company that also owns hospitals and medical clinics. I call it the BOX because you don't call your doctor, you call the BOX. Then the BOX calls your doctor because he doesn't have time for peasants like you and he tells the BOX what to say to you. The fun thing about the BOX is that you never know who you are talking to and it is very very rare that you would get the same person if you called again. It's like real life 50 First Dates because you get to tell your deep dark medical secrets to total strangers over and over and over and over. So I called the BOX and the conversation went something like this:

> **ME:** *Hello I am going on a trip next week and I am all out of Xanax and need them to fly.*

> **The BOX:** *Ok peasant, I will send a message to the doc and he has 48 hours to respond to you.*

> **ME:** *Ok, well if you could let him know that it's really important, I would appreciate it.*

> **The BOX:** *Not likely.*

And then I waited. After 48 hours I hadn't heard back from the BOX so I got the privilege of talking to a computer who connected me to the BOX.

ME: *Yes I left a message 48 hours ago and haven't heard back.*

The BOX: *It looks like Dr. Toogoodforyou has you scheduled for an appointment in 2 weeks.*

ME: *That's funny cause I need some Xanax this week.... (explains situation) and so 2 weeks doesn't work.*

The BOX: *Xanax is a controlled substance and we don't just hand it out like candy.*

ME: *Oh yes you do, I've seen full Nightline episodes about it.*

The BOX: *Ok, I will send this message and as you know he has 48 hours to respond.*

ME: *My flight is in 72 hours so this is important.*

The BOX: *(hangs up phone).*

And then I waited. After 48 hours I hadn't heard back and each and every therapeutic technique I had learned was flying like torpedoes out of my bag of tricks as the *holy crap I'm not gonna have any Xanax* took over. By this point I thoroughly hated the BOX and I was not afraid to show it (wow did I just say I'm not afraid?). Which remember the whole 'don't fight anxiety with fear' thing. You can, however, fight anxiety with anger. Once again, I called the computer and the computer connected me to the BOX.

> **ME:** *GIVE ME THE DRUGS (foaming at the mouth).*

> **The BOX:** *You're a drug addict!*

> **ME:** *I'M NOT A DRUG ADDICT, NOW GIVE ME THE @#$%^ DRUGS NOW!!!!!!!!!!!*

This went on for a while and I got transferred from one BOX rep to another. There may or may not have been some ugly crying, wailing, and gnashing of teeth from my end of the phone. Finally a soft voice came on.

> **The BOX:** *(whispers) Hey, are you there?*

> **ME:** *(barely alive) yes.*

> **The BOX:** *I too suffer from a fear of flying.*

ME: *Oh my goodness you're human! I'm finally talking to a human!*

The human in the BOX: *Yes, I ran upstairs and got the doc to sign off on a 3 pill script but you'll have to come in after your trip for more.*

ME: *(tears of joy) My children shall sing your praises all the days of their lives I give you my word.... . by the way, I'm not a crack whore.*

So I finally got my "fix" and was as ready as I would ever be for death—I mean the flight. The next 24 hours were a bit of a blur, partly because I drugged myself and partly because all the deep breathing was making me lightheaded. I don't take Xanax often enough to have a tolerance so I know that a safe level for me is just one pill. This means that I have to time that pill very *very* carefully. You see, the pill does not knock me out. I still feel fear and anxiety like I did before, but my nervous system can't respond so the wailing and screaming and freaking out happens only in my head—how ironic is that, 'it's all in my head. ' So I typically take the pill as we are walking down the ramp to board the plane. This allows maximum flying time with muted reactions. The downside is that I am full on, full feeling anxious in the airport and because of our lovely airport systems we have been advised to get there at least 2 hours early. If I wasn't so frightened and concentrating on deep breathing then I would so love to watch the other people around me. I am certain that every one of them is praying.... praying that they do not have the seat next to me! Imagine feet tapping, big deep (consequently loud) breaths, eyes closed, and every once in a while drips of tears rolling down my face. My sweet sweet husband has sat by me every time. Every. Single. Time. And I am sure that he can think of a million things he'd rather be doing than politely mouthing apologies to all the moms trying to distract their children or frequent flyers annoyed at the disturbances. My own children, who were on this trip with us, are quite used to this spectacle and probably think it's normal. I'm grateful Drew's a therapist so we can use our savings for their college and not their psych ward bills later in life.

During the flight I think I told Drew and the flight staff at least 10 times that I don't even want to go to Hawaii, that I hate Hawaii, and that I am positive I would be having way more fun at home doing laundry and dishes. Luckily because the Xanax relaxes my muscles, including my facial muscles, I got passed off as a drunk and not a psycho. It's amazing how fast 6 hours of binge watching a show on Netflix can fly (pun intended) and how slow 6 hours of internal anxiety and outward drunkenness lasts. By the time we were landing, the Xanax had definitely reached its half-life. I was able to keep it together—mostly by holding my breath—as we got closer and closer *and closer* to the ground. My thought turned from falling out of the sky in a long horrible death to please let the landing gear be functioning. BUMP. BUMP. SCREECH. WOOSH. Ah. We made it. Cue the ugly crying/laughing blotchy cheeks. *Take that anxiety, BOOYAH!* Hawaii was great. It smelled great. It felt great. It was definitely better than staying home and doing chores. The fear and anxiety, which I'll admit irrational fear and anxiety—which I am pretty sure all of us with anxiety will admit after the fact when all is good that it was irrational—did not keep me from living life and enjoying life. Just as an amputee who loves to run must modify how they accomplish their goals, so do I. In fact, it's kind of exciting in a weird masochist I-would-rather-not-deal-with-it kind of way.

So do I love flying now? No, but I do it when life necessitates. I have that choice each and every time I want to travel somewhere. I can give up and give in to my anxiety and say things like, "it's just not worth the hassle," and "I don't have the energy for the battle right now," or I can take the tools that I have been taught, along with a little blue pill and drag my butt onto that plane. Some of you may be thinking, "that's easy for her to say." If that is you then you need to go back and reread this chapter. It is incredibly hard for me to say and even harder for me to do. I surround myself with people who do not let me give up and I come to terms with the fact that there is going to be public crying involved. You live your life, don't let anxiety live your life.

CHAPTER 2: ANIMALS

"What counts is not necessarily the size of the dog in the fight - it's the size of the fight in the dog."
-Dwight D. Eisenhower

Hey, you're still reading. That's so sweet. I love animals....... in cages, really big ethical cages. I love that they complete the food chain and that because of animals we have food and clothing, and some of them eat bugs while others are really pretty. I love photos of animals in serene valleys and on top of high mountains. I love stories about animals that save people and I love that animals help sad people become happy and angry people become calm. I just don't want them anywhere near me, by me, within sprinting distance of me, or within a day's travel of me (animals at the zoo

excluded for obvious reasons). Unfortunately I have found that I am alone in my principles.

> *"I think that people who don't like animals tend to be selfish, but I'm biased."* **-Jessica Alba**

> *"Until one has loved an animal, a part of one's soul remains unawakened."* **-Anatole France**

> *"Four legs good, two legs bad."* **-George Orwell**

> *"Animals are such agreeable friends, they ask no questions, they pass no criticism."* **-George Eliot**

And the list could go on and on. I've tried
to figure out through the years why it is exactly
that I don't like animals. I guess I should mention
that there are a few exceptions: butterflies, baby
bunnies, and kittens, but cats are still on the bad
list. My family had animals periodically throughout
my life, so it wasn't that I was never exposed to
them—although if you want to psychoanalyze me,
I remember as a young child coming home from
school and running straight to my bed because
the puppy wasn't big enough to jump on my bed
(this also might be a reason why I love my bed so
much). One conclusion that I came to was that you
cannot understand nor reason with them. Some of

you animal lovers are chomping at the bit (haha another pun intended) to tell me that the same could be said of humans. And you are probably right, but anxiety is not about rational thoughts and fears. I remember when I had my first baby— yes this will relate—and a group of ladies came over to my home to congratulate me. They were holding my sweet 2-week old baby girl when she started to cry. One of the ladies turned to me and said, "What does she need?" I almost responded, "Seriously? How the crap would I know?" But of course my reaction was more polite and I said, "You know, I'm not really sure." She then told me, "Oh you'll learn and then one day you will know what she needs by her cry." I have now had 4 babies and to this day I do not speak baby cry. My guess is as good as yours. I keep trying things (change diaper, feeding, holding, etc) until I hit the right answer. *I thought she said this was going to relate?* The point is, I don't like animals because their language doesn't make sense to me and while human babies don't either, God blessed me enough to not be afraid of my own babies.

Think about it: when a dog barks I hear anything from "he just wants to say hi" or "don't come near she's protecting her territory" or "he just wants to smell you" (disturbing in its own way) to "she's just protecting me." How can you tell if the dog wants to kill you, or lick you, or pounce on you, or disturbingly smell you? In my mind it's a lot like football. When I watch football with my husband and he all of a sudden says, "are you kidding me, come on ref!" and I am like, "what happened?" and he says, "didn't you see that? The guy on the right face masked the other guy." *Sorry Drew that I can't remember what guy is on the right, cornerback? Defensive end? Receiver?* And they play the replay and clear as day—and in slow slow motion—I can see the guy face masking. I know that there are clues as to "what the dog is saying:" if the dog's tail is wagging, if the hair on the back of their necks is up, if their teeth are showing, and how the tongue is placed. But unless it's in slow motion on replay, all I get is bark bark= certain death. It also boggles my mind when a dog comes barking and running towards me and their owner says, "don't worry, she won't hurt you." Well she has a very scary way of *saying* that. All signs are pointing to "yes she will" from here. And this is just one example: Birds, horses, cats, bears, moose, and lizards are all worse communicators than even the dog!

Fortunately, for Drew and my kids, I did "get over" most of my fear of dogs and I had to go all the way to South America to do it. I lived in Uruguay on a proselyting mission for a year and a half. There are so many great things about the places and people of South America, but their views and laws on animals are very different. I don't remember seeing a dog on a leash. I do however remember seeing hoards and hoards of dogs on the street. And since they belong to no one, no one is responsible for training them to be nice. It was virtually impossible to go outdoors and avoid the dogs. So I had two options: stay inside and never get anything done and be safe, or venture out into the dog streets of Uruguay—and in my mind be eaten alive. Neither option was something that I wanted but after thinking about it, I finally found something deep within me that would "cure" me: Anger. Pure, teeth-clenching anger. I know how ironic this sounds since I was proselyting a gospel of love and peace, but "for every action there is an opposite and equal reaction" I guess. I had decided that every time I saw a dog and started to panic, I would consciously and fervently turn that fear into anger and I would make that dog fear me more than I feared it (calm down I am not a violent person, I'm all bark and little bite—hehe, I'm on a roll!). I was wondering what it would look like to have this sweet, well mannered, Sunday dressed lady walk down the street barking and growling at the dogs, but lucky for me the Uruguayans have trained their (collective street) dogs to be very very afraid of a kissy sound. No you read that right. You put your lips together, pucker up, and loudly kiss the air and the dogs run away. To spare my sweet Uruguayan friends from any PETA backlash, I'll bury the stories that I heard as to why the dogs are afraid of that sound. What sweet justice that I'm afraid of dogs saying "hello" and dogs are afraid of the prospect of a kiss from me! So while you can't fight anxiety with fear, you can fight it with anger. :) Healthy, happy, targeted anger. While I still don't enjoy dogs, I think it may shock you to know that Drew and the kids have a dog, that I let live in the house with us. I told you I'm a good person.

I was so glad to be empowered to take over my fear of dogs, but unfortunately that didn't translate to all other animals. This is mostly because I haven't been forced to interact with other species of animals on a day-to-day basis. Go ahead and include my dog stories as proof of the "overexposure" therapy methods. One of my favorite things is when someone tells you that you don't *have* to be afraid of something. I have anxiety, not a learning disability. I am aware that I, too, enjoy the freedoms of living in America and therefore "don't have to" do many things. When most people find out that I am terrified of deer, they will follow with "you don't have to be afraid of deer, they won't hurt you" and they are wrong. Very *very* wrong.

I was on a run one afternoon in the suburbs of Denver. It was a run through a neighborhood, an eastern neighborhood nowhere near the mountain. As I rounded a corner, a young (lost) buck looked up at me. I stopped and stared at the deer while he stared right back. I started to back away when instead of running the other way, like EVERYONE said it would, the deer started chasing me—Full on chasing me! Lucky for me, there was a school bus nearby waiting to pick up kids for the day. I knocked on the door and I'm pretty sure I sounded like the big bad wolf from *The Three Little Pigs:* "Let me in, let me in!" This poor bus driver was wondering if she was the next Dateline primetime story, but I guess she was either caught off guard or curious enough because she opened the door and I leapt inside to quickly shut it behind me. I told her that there was a ravenous—may have stretched the truth a bit, but I was terrified—deer after me. The conversation went something like this:

Me: *There is a ravenous deer after me!*

Driver: *A deer?*

Me: *Yes, a deer!*

Driver: *Wait, are you sure it was a deer? It wasn't a coyote?*

Me: *(stable enough to roll my eyes) I know what a deer is. It was a deer.*

At that point, the deer rammed into the bus door over and over.

Me: *Told you.*

The startled bus driver called it in to the district office and they said that sometimes in mating season, young deer can be aggressive. *Whaaat?* Turns out we humans do have a lot in common with deer. Because I don't have the time to roam the woods during mating season to find out if the kissy sounds works on deer too, I just make sure that there is someone slower than me when we go hiking.

Speaking of hiking... Even with my terrifying deer encounter, I love the smell of the mountains. I love the budding blossoms in the spring and the roaring rivers in the summer. I love the decaying leaves in the fall and the overwhelming pine smell in the winter. Unfortunately for me, deer really are the least of my worries when it comes to what else calls the forest its home. Because I have a problem identifying pheromones, I am never really sure whose territory I am on.

The best way to explain it to my fearless friends is to imagine the forest being divided by countries. You wanna go on a hike and you know that North Korea owns some land up there, as well as Russia, Venezuela, and a host of other countries who don't like the US. You happen to be an American. You've heard of other Americans being attacked, and while it's rare, there are YouTube selfie videos of them barely escaping. You have no way of knowing where the borders are. You really still want to go so you pack your North Korea spray (which everyone knows doesn't work and just pisses them off), your bells (because you don't want to startle the Russians—rumor has it they are kind as long as they aren't startled), and you take some friends with you (at least one that's slower than you because you know that the Venezuelans are fast). On this hike across the territories you see a Canadian in the distance. You know that they are peaceful—or at least you haven't seen YouTube death videos about them—and besides it's a safe distance away up on a cliff. So you take a picture and point out the Canadian to fellow hikers. You're secretly hoping that you hear an Australian because you love the sounds they make,

but not a whole cluster of them because Alfred
Hitchcock pretty much ruined that for you. Most
of the fellow hikers are really enjoying themselves,
and you are too, except in the not so back of your
mind is a hyper sensitivity to anything that could
remotely resemble a North Korean, a Russian, or
a Venezuelan. This is because you are a hateful
person. Wrong. This is because you want to obey
the rules and respect the borders, but you have no
way of knowing if you are doing that. Ok, you have
a few little clues, but they are easy to miss.

If I could see the future and know that
everything turned out as planned, (yup, the root
of all anxiety) I could run and frolic and enjoy the
Canadian and the Australian, and even the Russian
because I would see that we didn't die. But since
I can't, I mean you can't...this story is about you,
then you have to be keenly aware at all times. One
interesting thing about anxiety is this: while I know
that worrying about something doesn't reduce
the risk of something bad happening, this well-
intentioned advice from family, friends, doctors,
strangers, and flight attendants does not help one
single eency weency bit. I'm not worrying about a
Russian attacking me in the woods because I think
that it will feel my vibe and the reverse psychology
will make it change its mind: "Well if she's just

waiting for me to attack that's no fun at all, I guess I'll go get the unsuspecting one." No, I'm worried because I'm scared and it spills out of my body in the form of nail biting, sweating, antsy feet, angry responses—also known as "worry."Lucky for me I have a husband who is an outdoor fanatic. That, combined with his training in Psychology makes it nearly impossible for my anxiety to talk him out of a day in the woods, and in the end when it was a great day and we didn't die, I'm really glad that we went. I feel like at this point I should put a disclaimer that if you are reading this and I did die trying an adventure with Drew, I do not hold him legally or ethically responsible (nothing but love Sweetie!).

One thing that I have learned through the years is that "behavior precedes motivation." When I am out hiking, I am not always enjoying myself. I make a point of taking lots and lots of pictures and videos. That way, when I am safe at home, I can go back and look and watch and truly enjoy the experience. Through pictures,I can see the smiles on my kid's faces or the beauty of the fall leaves without worrying about when it is going to be dark or whether we will get lost. *Why would she do that? That sounds crazy.* With every positive experience, even if it is after the fact in pictures and videos, I am storing the positive feelings associated with hiking so that I am more and more motivated to go out in the woods. If I wait around to have more positive feelings than scared feelings before I try to go out.... I will never go.

CHAPTER 3: WEATHER

*"Everybody talks about the weather, but
nobody does anything about it."*
-Charles Dudley Warner

I love the stars. *She has a weird way of
introducing weather.* I always have. As a young
girl I would lay on the trampoline with my sister
and brothers all night long and stare at the stars.
We would look for shooting stars and pick out
the satellites. We would make shapes in the stars
and pretend that we knew which ones were
constellations. My first boyfriend in High School
stole my heart by "purchasing a star" and naming
it after me, which I am pretty sure would not hold
up at NASA but it was High School and deeply
romantic. Stars are one of the main reasons I
sought to live in the country where when the
sun goes down, the stars actually come out. I

convinced my parents to buy Drew a really nice telescope as a graduation gift mostly for him (ya right, mostly for me!) when he got his Master's. When I am at my favorite place on earth, Redfish Lake Idaho, the stars are so abundant and bright that the Milky Way actually looks like a river of milk with star flowers speckling the fields around it. It is almost overwhelming and definitely breathtaking. Stars represent peace to me. Stars mean no clouds and, consequently, no deadly weather.

Unlike animals that you must leave your house to seek out, weather comes and attacks you where you are. I hate it all: snow, rain, wind,

sleet, tornados, blizzards, hurricanes, flash floods, lightning, etc. Weather represents the ultimate in luck of the draw. It does not care how nice you are, how rich you are, or where you live. It strikes when and where it pleases. Meteorologists have become good guessers—ok, mediocre guessers at best, no offense—but they can't tell you which house on which street is going to be swept away by the tornado, washed away by the flood, broken by the downed tree, or lit on fire by the lightning. Since we have established how very smart I am, there is no need to emphasize that the odds of me dying in a freak weather related accident is a bajillion to one.

ANXIETY MAKES ME ANXIOUS

I could blame Hollywood for exacerbating my fear of weather with the likes of *Twister, Joe Versus the Volcano, The Day After Tomorrow, and The Perfect Storm,* but it also graced us with *Men In Black, Independence Day, and Prometheus* and I'm not afraid of aliens so there has to be another scapegoat. I blame the National Weather Service alerts. Just think: I'm in my house minding my own business, eating some cake, when all of a sudden I hear it. It starts off low and slow then gets loud and high. It's the dreaded alert siren, most associated with tornados. It's basically a honing beacon for all people with weather anxiety. It might as well be someone saying, "The end is near! Save yourselves!" Had I known that Denver was right smack in the middle of tornado alley—perhaps a slight exaggeration—I would not have moved there. So I guess in retrospect I am glad that I didn't know.

One horrible day there was a particularly scary storm. We lived in a little townhouse with a canal running behind it. The news stations warned us all day that there was a good chance of "severe weather," also know as "weather" to people like me. It had been hot and humid all day, which was clue numero dos that we were in for a bad one. We could see the storm clouds building from the north and coming south straight at us, which was strange because they usually went from the southwest to northeast. Drew grabbed a lawn chair and sat in the front lawn because he wanted to "watch the cool storm coming"and because he is just the right amount of redneck to do that. Drew is from Oklahoma so the Denver tornados made him laugh. I am from Idaho so the Denver tornados made me cry. Ok, you're right doesn't matter where I am from, all tornados everywhere make me cry, that ugly blotchy face cry with a few uncontrollable laughs of hysteria. I on the other hand was emptying our pantry because on the floor in the pantry was a door to the crawl space under the unit which was as close to a basement that I was going to get. Just as I had gathered the 72-hour kit and the windup flash lights, the sirens went off. I grabbed the kids and headed for the spidery crawl space, which the kids were not thrilled about. Given tornados versus spiders, I picked the spiders.

I could hear the rain pounding down on the windows and then the hail. Drew, by this point, had at least come to the front porch. In the middle of my fifth reciting of the Lord's prayer, Drew came over to the opening and said, "we may want to get upstairs." Was he nuts!? Everyone knows that you go to the basement for tornados, especially someone who actually *did* grow up in tornado alley. What I didn't know was that the bank of the canal had been breached because of the amount of rain we were getting, and because the hail had clogged the drain pipe. This breach was causing massive amounts of water to come towards the house. It was one of the hardest decisions I've had to make: stay in the crawl space and drown, or go upstairs and be taken by the tornado. I did the only logical thing that someone with weather anxiety in this situation would do: I threw everyone in the car and I was gonna get the hell out of there.

Our lovely little neighborhood had two entrances/exits...both on the same side of the subdivision.... both going out to the same street. This street had turned into a raging river because of the slope that it was on. So there we were, in the car with all the kids stopped at the raging river with the death sirens blaring in the background. At this moment I was having flashbacks, not to my own experiences but to videos on the news of cars being swept away in flash floods with the newscasters reminding everyone "that 6 inches of water is all it takes to cause you to lose control of your car and possibly stall it." *I really should stop watching the news, and TV in general but then how will I ever find out what Elizabeth's relationship to Reddington is??* So I turned to my kids and said,

"Well, this is it. Not how I pictured it but I love
y—" when Drew interrupted with, "Ok, mommy's
just being silly. Let's see if one of these neighbors
will let us in." Which they did and we were fine—
physically, but my kids still talk about that day so
I may or may not have aided in a little PTSD. The
irony of this is that a few years later when we were
deciding to move to Idaho "no tornados" was on
my "pros to moving" list and our very first summer
here there was a tornado warning. Like I said,
weather finds you.

I have proof that the National Weather Service
alert is to blame. Remember that time I was living
in Uruguay? Uruguay had its rainy season and
sunny season. One day in the sunny season I was
living near the coast—in fact I could walk to the
beach in less than 5 minutes. We didn't have a TV
so whatever "news" we got came in the form of
overhearing another person's conversation. In all
the conversations I overheard, I don't remember a
single one about a huge major storm about to hit
us. I had been out all day and the winds were really
starting to pick up. Then came the rain. Many of
the houses in Uruguay have metal roofs and when
it rains it sounds like God playing drums over the
house. It was getting dark and with it being nearly
impossible to hear inside the houses, we decided

to go home. Our house was lucky enough to have clay tile roofing. We filled up some empty bottles with water in case the storm stopped the water system from working, which it did, and made some dinner. We settled into bed as we listened to the storm intensifying. Every once in a while through the howling winds we would hear the crash of a clay tile. There was no way of knowing if it was one of our own tiles or the tiles of a neighbor's house flying off their roof. We could hear trees in the distance crashing sometimes to the ground and sometimes hitting houses. There was a difference in the *thud* that it made. I know that I was concerned, but I would call it a "normal" level of concern as I did fall asleep that night. What I don't remember hearing is a warning siren, because there was none. I'm not sure what a warning siren would have done for us anyways other than let us know that it was worse than we thought it was. When we went out the next morning, there were so many trees; trees and mud. We spent the better part of a week helping people clear trees from the roads and yards, and cleaning up everything that got wet and muddy from the relentless sideways rain. I still don't know to this day if it was a hurricane or a tropical storm but naming it didn't make much of a difference as far as the work that had to be done.

To contrast that story, let me tell you about a road trip to Arizona. I was living in Denver at the time and I really wanted to visit my sister and her family in Phoenix. This was during our poor grad student stage, as opposed to our poor undergrad stage and our poorer just graduated starting a business stage, so we had to drive. Drew had class so I undertook the adventure on my own. My lovely mother heard of my impending suffer-age so we worked it out where she would fly and meet me in Albuquerque and then finish the drive to Phoenix with me. The drive from Denver to Albuquerque went off without a hitch. We spent the night and picked my mom up at the airport the next morning. For anyone who has not driven from Albuquerque to Phoenix, let me help you. Think of all the images and movies you have seen about Area 51. Now take away the government buildings and the prospect of seeing an alien, and that is what the drive is like. Luckily, and thanks to smartphones, the National Weather Service alerts travel with you. It was a beautiful sunny day and my mom and I were deep in conversation when both of our phones starting alarming. My heart rate went up about 50 bpm as I asked my mom what was going on. Because she has been my mom my whole life, she tried to blow it off as nothing, and because I have been her daughter my whole life I knew exactly what she was doing. I finally got her to read the alert which was something to the effect of "huge and dangerous wind/sand storm in the area. Take shelter immediately." Take shelter? *Take shelter!!?? Where in the desert would you take shelter?* If they knew I was on that freeway then they should have known there was nowhere to hide. A "turn around and drive the other way" or "take your next exit heading south" would have been much more welcome advice. I still can't figure out how I had no cell coverage to be able to make a call or look on my google maps to find out what flippin' county I was in so I could see how close the sand death trap was, but the National Weather Service alert could still track me down. One of the cruelest things for someone with weather anxiety is to tell them that something's coming, that it's big, and that it could kill you when you're driving in some random county in an unfamiliar state. This is the exact reason I refuse to drive anywhere between the Rocky Mountains and the Appalachian Mountains between April and October (tornados). I refuse to do it between October and April for blizzards and ice storms. There was a lot of anxiety in that car for the remaining 3 hours of that drive and I did not see one tiny grain of sand blow past my windshield. Thank you National Weather Service alerts for that lovely ride.

So how do I ever live life with my fear of weather? I find that the saying "if ye are prepared ye shall not fear" is incomplete. I would add "... but if ye are too prepared and have anxiety then ye shall fear". Weather cannot be changed by preparation. While it is a good idea for me to have a general sense of what the weather will be like—so I am wearing appropriate clothing or have necessary equipment i. e. an umbrella—it is better for me to have the quick onset of anxiety that I can deep breath through, versus hours or even days to snowball that anxiety into a full on panic attack. If I don't know about the mole hill it makes it harder to build that mountain.

Through my years of avoiding weather I have become quite good at spotting clouds, watching how they form and which direction they are headed in. I can determine rotation in clouds that even the Dopplers can't see. Amazingly I've learned to enjoy some weather, the kind with very minimal risk. I prefer a slow drizzly day to a quick hitting fire hose storm. I enjoy soft falling snow flakes versus sideways blinding whiteouts. I think a lightning storm in the far far distance has marks of true beauty. And above all, I am pushing through the fear of a possible weather catastrophe and getting on with my life—with my 72-hour emergency kit in tow—every single day.

CHAPTER 4: TUNNELS, CAVES, & ELEVATORS

"Lost my ideals in that tunnel of time."
-Jim Croce

The saying "there is a light at the end of the tunnel" rings truer to someone who has a phobia of enclosed spaces than anyone else. People react to fear usually in one of three ways: They either fight, run away (flight), or freeze. While I am usually a "freezer," I like to keep my options open so when "flight" is taken off the table, I feel a lot of anxiety. There is a tunnel on I-70 about an hour west of Denver that is essential for getting to many of the hiking and camping places that we love, as well as many of the ski resorts. This tunnel is the Eisenhower Tunnel and as a result, Eisenhower is my least favorite president of all time. The tunnel is

about 1. 7 miles long. At a speed of about 55 mph it takes approximately 1 minute and 48 seconds to get through it. This is a really long time for me to hold my breath and impossible for me to close my eyes since I am usually the one driving—Have I shared that I get seriously car sick if I don't drive? *And yes, getting car sick often makes you very popular in high school.*

One thing that Eisenhower and his subsequent cronies have decided to do is put little lights, green circles and red "X"'s, every couple of yards in the tunnel. The excuse is that it helps traffic move to one side or the other if there is an accident in the

Colorado News Daily

Sept. 3, 2015

LOCAL WOMAN TRAPPED IN TUNNEL

authorities determine that rescue attempts 'probably aren't really worth the effort'

"We went out and moved some rocks around but honestly we just have a lot of other things to worry about."
-Mayor Johnson

Friday evening, friends of local Shayna Brazier began receiving text messages complaining, 'It's dark in here,' 'is anyone coming,' and 'I'm so scared and I really have to pee.' Unfortunately city budget for search and rescue is limited after last month's chalk festival. "I try to remind people, you win some you lose some" the mayor commented. Saturday morning friends and family gathered

tunnel. Really, it's just a torture device for people who hate tunnels. It is a reminder every 5 seconds that there is a very real possibility that you could get in a wreck in the tunnel, or better yet that a wreck could happen ahead of you and you could be trapped in there until they figure out how to clear it. The whole drive through the tunnel I find myself saying "no wammies, no wammies" as we pass each marker. I usually prefer to drive in tunnels at night because I can pretend that we are indeed not in a tunnel but outside in the dark. In the daylight you have to take your sunglasses off in order to see in the tunnel which renders it virtually impossible to trick yourself at that point. The

Eisenhower tunnel has taken that trick away with their X's and O's. This tunnel however is preferred to the Carmel tunnel in Zion's National Park. While the Carmel tunnel has a friendlier distance of 1. 1 miles long, it has a hidden unwelcome surprise. Every so often in this tunnel there are cut-out "windows" that open to the canyon below. They are beautiful..... . if you weren't in a tunnel. But you are in a tunnel, so they are deceiving because you can see the light coming from them and if you are a novice driver in this tunnel, you would think that you were near the end. Nope! It's a trick, and a scary trick that not only reminds you that you are still in the tunnel, but also that there is a sheer cliff on the side of you, so you better hope those 80-year old engineering plans got their math right.

Like I have stated before, it's not the act of dying that is the most terrifying, it is the displeasure that precedes the dying that I would love to avoid. If the tunnel caved in and I was crushed to death, I don't think I would much care... since I would be dead. But if it caved in around me and I slowly dehydrated to death, then that... *that* I think I would hate. And better than death, but still totally embarrassing, is that I get trapped, they eventually get me out, but I was in there long enough that I couldn't hold it anymore and I am rescued in my own urine. Speaking of things caving in, caves create similar anxieties within me. The difference being that I usually have to backtrack my way out of a cave, not just get through it as fast as possible. When Drew and I were in Mexico for our 10-year anniversary I so badly wanted to experience the Cenotes. These are vast underground cave/water ways that you can explore and swim in. I was hesitant knowing that it would likely give me anxiety—and remember I had just endured a flight to get there, and an impending flight home. Drew used his excellent reasoning skills, along with some highly effective manipulating skills, to convince me to take the opportunity because I would regret not doing it. Drew and I both speak Spanish fluently though I rarely have the opportunity to use it—*truth be told I could create those opportunities even here in Idaho*—so when the guides were going over the safety rules and procedures, I was enamored at the way it sounded and found that calmed many of my nerves. It wasn't until we were under the ground crawling on our bellies that I started to panic. The water was cool enough under there that while I was quivering with fear I was able to pass it off as a shiver from being cold, and my hyperventilating passed as hypothermia. There were moments where we were able to turn off our lights and see how dark it really was, which took my breath away...in the bad way. I literally had a hard time breathing. But lucky for me there were children in our tour group so the "lights off" experiment ended quickly. Poor Drew puts up with a lot from me and my "disorder" but I think one of the hardest things is that I can't take full advantage of all of the romantic moments in life. Fearless Shayna would have been making out in that dark Mexican cave, but unfortunately fearless Shayna has rarely been seen on this planet. I think of all of the beautiful and quiet moments in life that could have been so very romantic but instead got spent dealing with the fears that flood my head when things are too quiet (We do have 4 kids though so don't feel too bad for us). I'm glad I went on that tour. It was a definite highlight on that trip—after we got out and we were safe.

Elevators have qualities that caves and tunnels have as far as me feeling trapped in a tiny space, but with the added excitement of plummeting to the ground. There is a ride at Disneyland called the Tower of Terror. I almost feel like I can stop there as it says everything I need to about elevators. This ride was literally taken out of my worst case anxiety scenarios play book. Whenever possible, and feasible, I take the stairs. As a funny twist of fate, my children LOVE elevators and beg to ride them all the time. Since obesity is on the rise, I definitely have the upper hand when it comes to my argument to walk versus ride but there are some buildings that are very *very* tall and my kids are very *very* small, so I have ridden on my fair share of elevators. I am one of the few people on this planet that truly appreciate elevator music. When there is a nice background tune it drowns out some of the metal on metal scraping and dinging that happens on every single elevator ride, which is the least comforting noise on the planet. Close your eyes and picture a scene from an action movie—ok, if you are reading this yourself then obviously keep your eyes open but pretend they are closed. In this movie there is a building that is about to collapse. The protagonist is trapped while the other protagonist fights to save their lives. Just as the building is on its teetering last breath, they narrowly escape doom and watch in horror what could have been their fate. Now what do you hear in the background while all of this is happening? That's right: the noises that an elevator makes on a normal everyday ride, especially an old elevator in an old building. Dying in an elevator is not very probable, and I can even admit that right before going on one, but getting stuck in an elevator is much more likely. Just to be cautious, I make sure that I use the ladies room before going on an elevator because the only thing worse than being trapped... is being trapped with no bathroom.

The thing about life is that I am always going to find myself in tight spaces either figuratively or realistically. I know that the tunnel, or the cave, or the elevator is a means of getting me somewhere and it's funny that so are hard decisions. They make you feel like you are being pushed on every side. For both scenarios I take a deep breath. That sounds simple, and it is. I take a deep breath, I channel my fear into anger, and I use that anger as the fuel I need to get through that experience. I refuse to let a passageway stand in between me and a place that I might love more than I had thought. When deep breathing and anger just don't quite do the trick, I go over the lines of a church hymn in my head. I had a teacher in high school once share with me the lines to a church hymn and how memorizing it helped her every time she was scared (I will not share this teacher's name because her advice has helped me so much in my life and it would be ludicrous for her to get in trouble for mixing church and state). The hymn reads:

Fear not, I am with thee oh be not dismayed
For I am thy God and will still give thee aid.
I'll strengthen thee, help thee, and cause thee
to stand.
Upheld by my righteous omnipotent hand.

Some of my scariest moments in life have been lived through with these words running in my head.

CHAPTER 5: HYPOCHONDRIA

"The hypochondriac disease consists in indigestion and consequent flatulency, with anxiety or want of pleasurable sensation."
-Erasmus Darwin

I'm not saying that I come from a line of hypochondriacs, but if I did then half of my relatives would agree with me and the other half are the ones with this disorder! Hypochondria is when you think you have whatever ailment those around you have, or anyone on the planet has ever had. Really, it's just a fear of having something medically wrong with you. Our bodies are amazing but our minds are even more amazing. We can literally tell our bodies to start having symptoms without even trying—trust me, I know. My ancestors must have had to work really hard at developing symptoms that were fake. They would

have had to know someone with a rare ailment or studied medicine in depth. Lucky for me, WebMD has solved that problem. WebMD is like a treasure chest for hypochondriacs. You can find any disease, even diseases and symptoms that you didn't even know existed. You could have a pain in your elbow and before you know it, you are setting up an appointment with your doctor to determine if it's a rare blood disease or Stage 4 elbow cancer. And never put something generic like "stomach pain" or "chest pain" because while logic says that it is gas and heartburn, WebMD says renal failure and parasites.

For the longest time I thought for sure I had a heart condition. This was just after my first panic attack. My heart would start racing for no reason at all and I would have what I called "heart hiccups," later diagnosed as a benign heart arrhythmia, which ironically is caused by anxiety—the gift that keeps on giving. My family has a deep history of heart attacks, both on my dad and my mom's side. Both of my biological grandfathers died of heart attacks before I was born. My paternal grandmother had a few heart attacks before passing of eventual "everything" failure. Two of my paternal uncles died of heart attacks at an early age so in my mind, it was only a matter of time until I got mine. I would feel pain in my chest and then go through the checklist: *Pain in my neck? Ya I think so. Wait, is my arm having pain? Is numbness in my hands a sign? What about pain in my back? Could it be a heart attack that is radiating to another part of me? Am I breathing shallow? Is there an "elephant" on my chest?* It got bad enough that several times I went to the ER and just sat in the parking lot in case it was a heart attack. I felt so stupid because logic said I was fine. I was exercising regularly and eating a healthy diet, besides I was young. I had many appointments with doctors for my pregnancy and heart issues were never brought up, but just in case, I kept a detailed log of my blood pressure so they could put it in my chart when I got my heart attack. Still I couldn't shake the fear. Lucky for me I do not have agoraphobia, which is the fear of being in public (social anxiety), mostly because you might have a panic attack. I actually experienced the exact opposite. I would stay out all day long until I knew Drew would be back home so that if I were to have a heart attack, someone would see me and help me. I didn't want to have a heart attack in private and then have my babies trapped in the house for hours with no supervision—remember death is not the worst case scenario. So I walked. I walked for hours every day, sometimes with friends, sometimes alone but always within sight of at least one other person. I also honed my browsing through Target skills during this time. The good news is that all of that walking probably would have prevented any heart attack that was looming and even though it wasn't the goal at the time, I lost a little bit of weight too. I guess it's like positive peer pressure where you get good consequences for something that is normally bad.

One particular time I had a severe headache that wouldn't go away. Knowing what I know now, it was probably a migraine, but I had never had one before so of course I thought I was dying. I was nervous enough about it that I went to my cousin Jen's house so she could watch the kids while I went to the ER. My sweet cousin Jen probably knew I was crazy and that I didn't need to go to the doctor, like the many times before, but she was so nice that she just supported me without judgment. The ER doc on the other hand was not as kind. When I would go to the ER I would try to act as if whatever was bothering me wasn't really a big deal because through all my craziness I still had the human desire to be "normal." I casually strolled into the waiting room and as calmly as I could I said, "Hey I have this headache, it's really not a big deal—" *Other than the fact that it might be a tumor or a blood clot or worse* "—I really think a baby aspirin would do the trick." I am such a dork. I know that triage nurse was thinking, *Why did I do that many years of schooling for a baby headache?* But since they have to, they took my name and I waited. When it was my turn to be seen, the doctor had me explain what was going on. He was young and probably brilliant and definitely annoyed with me. I don't blame him—I was annoyed with me. After checking my vitals he said, "Well there are two options here: I can give you a shot of steroids that will definitely make your headache go away but it will keep you up all night, or you can get a cat scan to make sure it's not something more serious." And then he looked at me, disgustingly. Me, trying to appeal to his egotistical side asked, "Well, what would you do if you were me?" thinking he would be honored that I wanted his opinion. What followed is on the top 10 of my most embarrassing/degrading moments of my life thus far. He said, "I would not be at the ER over something as non-life threatening as a headache so I don't even know what to tell you." There it was. Confirmation that I, indeed, was a freak."Normal" people don't go to the ER for a headache."Normal" people don't think that a headache means impending doom. I took the steroid shot and had all night to think about what a loser I was. I cried a lot that night.

I can't remember the exact moment that my hypochondria lessened. It still rears its head every once in a while, but I am rarely seen at the ER these days. I think it was a combination of things that got me through it. The first one was anger. There came a point where I was angry enough at feeling stupid that I had decided, "You know what, fine. So what if I die. So what if I have a heart attack right here and right now." I remember sitting in my apartment a couple of these times and making myself stay in the house, versus going outside so someone could see me, just to prove to myself that I was stronger than this fear. A little bit of my anger was pointed at God and I would have chicken matches with Him in my head where I would say, *Ok, I'm ready. I'm not playing. Give me a heart attack, I dare you.* While I would like to go on record here on earth, *and also on the records of Heaven,* as saying my anxiety is not God's fault and I do not condone being angry with God as a means of "healing" it... it kinda worked. On those days nothing happened. I did not have the impending heart attack I thought I was going to have, or the stroke, or the brain aneurysm—yes, I know this is obvious since I am typing this right now. I did, however, gain strength.

When I feel certain physical sensations and my natural reaction is to start thinking of all the things that could be wrong with me, I take a deep breath and I am reminded of some of those days and I more easily deal with the fear.

The second thing that I felt helped was using my fear and anger for good. I had decided that I was going to help people who were dealing with the actual medical things that I was afraid of having. I started by donating blood. I liked to think of it as my "supplemental health insurance." I had decided that if I did good medical deeds, bad medical things wouldn't happen to me, like karma. This is not scientifically true by the way (I did end up having an emergency appendectomy a few years back) but why not let my irrational thoughts lead to something positive for a change. So I donate blood. This is not easy for a hypochondriac to do. Here is how my most recent blood donating session went.

I usually donate blood at the gym where I work out. They have them every 6 months or so, so it's convenient, plus I can drop the kids off at the in-house daycare. I decided to get a little workout in before I donated because I was traveling the next day, so I knew I'd be sitting on my butt a lot. I went down to fill out the paperwork and I realized that I was feeling pretty hungry. They have snacks there on the table but they are for people after they donate. I weighed my options. I could grab a snack now and try to explain to the volunteer that I had just worked out and that I think a snack would be good before I donate blood so that I don't get light headed. Then the thought occurred to me, *What if I am not supposed to eat before because the food could make me queasy—and then if I threw up that would be embarrassing, or worse... if I passed out and then threw up I could choke on my own vomit?* I decided against the snack. I had just worked out though, so I knew that I needed to drink water. I didn't want my veins to be deflated and hard to find because that would be painful. I grabbed the water bottle and drank the whole thing.

By this time it was my turn to go back into the "triage" at the blood drive. This is a very short medical check. They checked my blood pressure. *Oh good, not looking like a stroke today.* They checked my iron. *Looks like I'm not anemic.... today.* Then they have you answer a bunch of questions about diseases. This is particularly fun as I get to stockpile new diseases that I may not have today but could certainly have in the future. I try to glaze over those questions as fast as I can so that I have as little time possible to commit them to memory. I'm pretty sure that if I had some crazy disease that prevented me from donating blood, the doctors would have told me. The hard questions are about the people you come in contact with. Have you in the past 5 months come in contact with someone who has smallpox? *Small pox, small pox.... well the lady at Target had some funny marks on her neck, was that small pox? I can't remember was she coughing? Wait, didn't grandma just get a vaccine for smallpox? I wonder when I need my next booster for small pox? I should check into that.* And since there is no "maybe" answer on the questionnaire, I go with a "no." This goes on for a while getting into some funky questions about whether I've slept with a man who has slept with a woman who is sleeping with another man etc.

Once I was done with the questionnaire, they had me sign some paperwork stating that if I have HIV or a couple of other diseases they would be contacting me with those results. So that's nice that I get to have some anxiety for the next few weeks every time a number that I don't recognize calls my phone. They checked my arms for needle tracks to which I got a "you passed" smile from the nurse. Then she walked me over to the drip chair. This is where they drain your blood, a safe amount at a safe rate I am told. This is also where I start to get fidgety, partly because I am not a fan of needles and partly because I am thinking about all the things that could go wrong: passing out, not having my blood clot and having to get a transfusion of my own, the needle not going in right, etc. So I start telling myself that none of these things will happen because I am helping others—karma, remember?! The nurse then turns to me and asked me if I am allergic to iodine. I have never been allergic to iodine so the correct response would be no, but because I am hyper aware of medical things going wrong I do know that you can develop an allergy to something that was previously benign for you, and this is what they mean when they say too smart for your own good. I muster up my courage to say no, mostly because I think that if I tell the nurse that there is always a chance that today I am allergic that it might make her rethink having me as a donor, then I sit and stare at the iodine scrub being rubbed all around my arm hoping that I don't start swelling. This caught the eye of the nurse who asked again, "You said you aren't allergic to iodine right?" *Why is she asking me that again? Ugh, that's just going to make me more nervous.* So I just kept thinking *"karma karma karma"* and I answered her poignantly, "Nope, not allergic."

I was about half way filling the blood bag when that entire bottle of water that I chugged hit me. I started pumping the squishy ball that they put in my hand faster and faster to try and speed this thing along. Normally I take the entire 10 minutes that they ask you to wait to stay as close to the nurse as possible in case I have any negative reactions but the "urge" was strong enough that the minute she wrapped my arm, I jumped out of that chair and ran to the Lou. This further drives home the fact that most of my "medical" problems are in my head and could be cured with a more pressing, actual need.

So I know that it seems that my "cure" actually makes my anxiety worse, but it gives me practice in a controlled environment, where I don't have to pay. I practice telling my anxiety that I am in control of my reactions, and while it might control some of my physical responses, I control what I am going to do about it.

The third thing—*oh ya, she was telling us things that helped her anxiety geez she got off track*—that helped my medical anxiety was money, or lack thereof. The ER is really expensive, even for just a baby aspirin. While this book is not political in nature, let's just say that the Affordable Care Act was not so affordable for us and we just couldn't afford my hypochondria any longer. So I guess in a weird twisted way, the ACA helped me overcome some of my anxiety.

CHAPTER 6: EVERYDAY LIFE

*"Truth is a deep kindness that teaches us to
be content in our everyday life."*
-Kahlil Gibran

I know that I have narrowed in on some of
my biggest anxiety triggers but truth be told, I
have many many more little ones. The only thing
that I have "officially" been diagnosed with is
Generalized Anxiety Disorder. This is probably true
for the majority of you with anxiety. I could easily
avoid planes, animals, weather (not as easily),
tunnels, and sick people, but I would still find
things to be anxious about. That's one of the hard
parts: it could be the clearest day in a calm place in
a relaxed environment, and I could find the "threat"
to my way of living. Let me walk you through what
some typical thoughts on a typical day might look
like for me.

I remember not too long ago I was driving home from the gym and I felt light headed. I had grabbed a bag of pretzels as I was leaving thinking that it might help. The kids of course thought that I bought the pretzels for them and each grabbed a handful. I told them that they needed to save me a few. Then my (9 year old) daughter asked why I needed the pretzels and I told her that I felt light headed and I didn't want to pass out. She then asked what they should do if I passed out and I told her that she would need to grab the wheel and steer us to a safe place. She responded, "Mom, I don't even have my learners permit, how am I supposed to do that?" To which my (7 year old) son responded, "It's ok, I'll jump over the seat and steer us to safety." At least I am teaching my children valuable problem solving strategies.

When I go to the grocery store I worry about not getting everything that I need, or getting too much and it going bad. I worry every single time that I check out that my card is going to get declined, even though that has only happened once in college because someone hacked into my bank account and drained the funds. *As a side note, this whole chip reader thing is not anxiety friendly. When it is time to take your card out it gives the "declined" beep beep that I have*

so dreaded my whole life. I have thoughts in my mind about a gunman coming into the store and which aisle I would hide in, which would probably be the health food isle—I just don't see a gunman knowing where the organic oats are. I think about the possibility of running into someone I know, but that I can't remember their name and how I would handle that—"Hey, you! Wow, you look great, what have you been up to?" Thoughts come into my head that aren't even related to the store, things like: *Did I leave the oven on? Is the garage door closed? Did my son take the lunch money I left out for him? What if it snows on Drew's drive home tonight and he gets in a wreck. Did I tell him I love him before he left? What if I am one of those people who have to tell everyone for the rest of their life how much they regret not telling their spouse they love them before they died?* Then I hurry and send an 'I luv u" text. It's kind of a miracle that I get enough groceries for a complete meal.

I have been getting more and more into running the past few years and have dabbled in a few trail races lately. These races are a great time to experience a combination of fears. I get to be up in the woods alone (sometimes I can keep up with others) with all of the beautiful uncaged animals. I get to feel my heart beat, loudly because these races are hard, and I get to talk myself out of a heart attack. I get to focus on the ground so I don't trip while simultaneously focusing on the clouds to see if there is any bad weather coming. I worry about the people around me and how I would react if they had an emergency. I worry about my kids who are either with a babysitter, if Drew is racing too, or with Drew, who is very capable and I am aware I shouldn't worry, and whether they are ok and if the baby has a clean diaper and I hope they haven't gotten lost and did they get fed. I worry about coming in last, not because I think I'm too good of a runner, but because animals usually pick off the slow and sick ones first—I never worry about coming in first! haha. I worry about making it to the next bathroom (I realize I have a lot of 'bathroom' anxiety, I wonder what Freud would say about that). I worry that I will hate running almost as much as I worry that I will love it, as running takes lots of resources: time, energy, money. Then a couple hours after the race when my heart slows down and I've had some time to decompress I end up signing up for another one.

I have anxiety for other people. I would hate for an experience to lack enough anxiety so I make sure that I cover the gap in case others aren't pulling their weight. When I see people perform, I am in awe of their talents while I also cringe at the thought of them messing up. I almost can't watch a solo singer because I want so badly for it to be a good experience for them that I hold my breath while they entertain me. I tense up when watching the auditions for reality talent shows because I don't want people to have to live with the shame of having the whole world watch them choke. No, I don't think I'm a saint who cares so deeply for others that it oozes out my pores, I think I'm an expert worrier and I can't help but use my talent at all times and in all things and in all places. I look forward to the day when I get my ultimate anxiety test and I get to watch my own children, whom I have invested time, money, and my body into, have their moments in the spotlight. Although, I did feel better about this when I watched the YouTube videos of the parents of the USA gymnasts (Aly) in the 2016 Olympics—Google it, this is literally how I feel anytime anyone performs.

I get anxious when I am with a new group of people for the first time. I worry about what they will say, how I will laugh, and what my role in that group will be. *Am I the funny one? Is there already a funny member? Would I offend that person or look like I'm trying to take their spot? Is there a smart one? Should I be the smart logical one? When they find out about my irrational fears will they think I was being fake? Should I be quiet and just see where I fit in? Oh, it's so hard for me to be quiet. If I'm too loud I could offend someone without knowing it and we all know how important first impressions are. Maybe I should just stay home.* I really think this is a big part of why people with anxiety choose to stay home; the pressure is high. No, in my heart of hearts I know I am a social person. I like people. Besides, I can always find a new group of people to experiment on if I totally muff this one up.

I worry about my kids.... a lot. I am sure that some of this is universal to every parent, everywhere but I like to think I go above and beyond. I worry about my parents and their health and safety because they travel a lot. I worry about Drew and how he is feeling and what kind of stress he might be under. I worry about my siblings and the struggles that they are going through, both the ones that I know about but more the ones that I don't. I worry about strangers and whether or not I could have been the person that smiled at them that "changed their whole life." I worry about my leaders, as well as people I have leadership over. I worry about the people who will read this book (all 5 of you, hey!) and whether my 'advice' is going to help or hurt and whether that will lead to friendships, or being sued, and whether that will lead to success or bankruptcy.

Sometimes anxiety can be very random. It was late one night when the wind started to pick up outside. I asked my husband if he had secured the hot tub lid from sitting in it earlier. He said that he did, but the thought that the lid might blow off kept coming back to me. I couldn't shake it, so when Drew went to the bathroom I snuck outside to check the lid for myself. Sure enough, he had latched it down just fine. We started to watch a show and the wind got a little more intense. I asked Drew if he thought we needed to secure the lid better and he casually said no. I don't remember a lot of the show that night. I do remember fighting my urge to go check the lid every 10 minutes.

We went to bed that night and the wind had not subsided. I woke up about 3am in a sheer panic because I just knew that the lid had flown off. I jumped out of bed, which woke Drew up. As I was putting on my shoes to go chase the lid down, Drew asked what I was doing and since I was tired and so sure that the lid was gone I answered, "I'm going to get that stupid lid that I knew we should have secured better" and I stormed off. About 2 minutes later I shamefully opened the door and crawling back into bed. Drew asked, "The lid was fine, right?" and I said "yes," and we went back to sleep.

I love speaking Spanish. My mom asked me one day if I wish I would have been born a Mexican. This made me laugh, and then made me wonder, *Maybe I do.* I studied Spanish in High School and then in College. I majored in Spanish Teaching for a while. I lived in Ecuador for 6 months, working in an orphanage, huge plug for OSSO—Google it. And then I lived in Uruguay for a year and a half. I love hearing the Spanish words roll off my tongue. I love listening to music in Spanish and I love eating Mexican food. I may have creeped a few Hispanic people out by leaning in too close to follow their personal conversations just because I wanted to hear the words. I have taught Spanish classes before to fellow *gringos.* When I am with a native Spanish speaker, I have an enormous amount of anxiety. I want so badly to communicate with them, and I am worried that when I start speaking Spanish they will not understand me and my whole life's worth of studying—ok, half-life's worth of studying—will have been a failure. I worry that I will forget a word and it will get me flustered enough that I will revert back to English and pretend that I didn't actually know Spanish. I start getting butterflies in my stomach when I am at a school, a check stand, or a library, and a native Spanish speaker is struggling to communicate their need while the English speaker on the receiving end is struggling to understand, and I want so badly to jump in the middle like Superman coming to save the day. Sometimes I build up the courage in time and sometimes I don't. When I do, it is pure Euphoria. When I don't, classic disappointment.

So how do I help my everyday anxiety? I have made the conscience decision that I am in control of my life. I decide what I am going to do and where I am going to do it. I cannot control whether or not anxiety will tag along, which it usually does because I think it's pretty clear that I am super fun to be around. It's almost as if I treat my anxiety like an actual other entity. I make a decision about an everyday task; for example, I decide that I would like to go bowling that particular day. Then I ask myself if I didn't have anxiety would I still choose this activity? *Yes, bowling is awesome.* I then say to my anxiety, which I really should give her a name, and yes she's a girl but only because how creepy would that be to have a boy following me around all day? *I am doing this thing and if you insist on being there then fine.* I fight— yes, I said *fight* to retain the power to choose for myself what I will and will not do. Being stubborn is not inherently evil. It can be incredibly powerful. Be stubborn. If you need help with this, please hang out with a 3-year old for a few days.

CONCLUSION: YOLO

"I'm fairly certain that YOLO is just Carpe Diem for stupid people."
-Jack Black

It's true. You really do only live once. Some of you may be asking what you can do to help your loved one, or acquaintance, or stranger who has anxiety. It's simple. Give them a hug, but not an awkward 'I'm-so-sorry-you-are-so-dysfunctional' kind of hug. Give them the 'You-got-this-and-you-have-so-many-awesome-qualities-that-outweigh-your-anxiety' kind of hug. Then let go, and push them to live their life. I don't think Drew—or my parents or siblings or friends or strangers or flight attendants—could count the times that I have yelled at them, mostly in Spanish so the kids don't understand, when they are "making" me do something that makes me anxious.

Equally, I don't think they could count the many times I have apologized and told them that I am so glad they pushed me to do scary things.

The second suggestion I would make is let them be angry. Anger overcomes fear. It really does, but don't worry because love overcomes anger so in the end, Love wins. Being angry is always viewed in such a negative way when there are some really positive things that anger can do. Anger gives you the drive you need to change things in your life. Anger helps you move forward, versus depression that helps you stay stagnant. Anger diverts attention from things that are scary. Anger gets things done when anxiety just can't. Let people be angry—in fact teach them to be angry in a healthy way, not in the destructive hurt people way.

The third thing I would say is let them "choose their own adventure." You are not in charge of deciding what someone with anxiety should or should not do. *Wait, didn't she say to push them to do things above?* Ask permission to be an agent for courage, but not in the moment of anxiety. If you are doing that, you are no more help than the anxiety itself. What's depressing is when someone or something else decides what you are going to do. Let your loved ones with anxiety pick their own

battles, and then push them in the battles they choose. Yes, this is frustrating. I find it incredibly frustrating when I have suggested a gift that my kids should ask "Santa" for and they flat out reject it. I know for a fact that the super cute ukulele would be 1000 times more useful and fun—and last longer—than the Monster High action figure, but because it has no bearing on my kids safety, I'm not going to erase her list and write mine in—Ok, maybe I did, but then I felt bad and let her write her own list again. Share your feelings, thoughts, and suggestions with people with anxiety just like you would with your "normal" kids/friends/lovers/

strangers and then react just as you would with the "normal" group when they blow you off.

While I shared some personal stories in a lighthearted nature, life has not always been a barrel of laughs. I know that anxiety is painful for many of you/us. Some of you may be able to share it, but not laugh about it yet, and you may not be able to for a while. Some of you who have known me for a long time are probably shocked to hear what was going on in my head for so many years; others of you are probably less shocked; while the majority of you are perhaps frightened to be around me now. Some of you are probably wondering if this is why Aunt Sally or Cousin John are so irritable all the time.

There are people all around us every day on this journey we call life that are passing through some hard things, much harder than the passages of my life that I've shared. Some people cope by expressing themselves. Some cope by shutting themselves in. Some of my biggest trials, I still can't talk openly about. Some of them I can write books about, non-therapeutic often rambling books. Time has a way of softening the horror and illuminating the pleasure of certain life experiences. Low times in life were once described to me as walking through a field of roses: While you are doing it, it's mostly thorns. They are cutting you and hurting you and you can barely see your way through them. You can smell a whiff of their sweet fragrance, but it is mixed with so many of your salty tears that it's hard to enjoy. Then, one day, you pop out of the field and look back to see the myriad of pedals in a symphony of colors. And you think, *You know, that wasn't so bad.* The scars heal and the pain fades. Anxiety can be painful, agonizingly painful, but when you come up for a second and see the tops of the roses, your life really is worth it. Get some true friends, get some real therapy, get some tissues, get angry, and then get on with the business of living. I often think about all the things and memories I would have missed out on if I didn't have a team of people around me pushing me to my boundaries, and sometimes shoving me over them. I think of all the memories my kids have of hiking and traveling and stupid elevator rides that could have so easily been replaced with staying at home with the doors locked because it was easier for mommy. I have been blessed beyond measure with my best friend and soul mate by my side. He is the steady helm that a crazy girl like me needs to steer my life into the sunset of success. Godspeed and good luck!

THE END

41102932R00058

Made in the USA
Middletown, DE
03 March 2017